THE Curmudgeon

THE Curmudgeon

A Guide for Men Over Sixty

Bob Eggers

SUNSTONE PRESS

SANTA FE

A special thanks to Joan Tewkesbury and
good friends Theo Raven and Patricia Eggers
for their wise counsel.
*

Sunstone books may be purchased for educational, business, or sales promotional use.
For information please write: Special Markets Department, Sunstone Press,
P.O. Box 2321, Santa Fe, New Mexico 87504-2321.

Book and cover concepts by Eric Jacobson
Body typeface › Candara
Printed on acid-free paper
∞

Library of Congress Cataloging-in-Publication Data

Eggers, Bob, 1932-
   The curmudgeon : a guide for men over sixty / by Bob Eggers.
      pages cm
   ISBN 978-0-86534-065-7 (softcover : alk. paper)
   1. Older men--Humor. I. Title.
   PN6231.M45E365 2013
   741.5'6973--dc23
                        2013043439

WWW.SUNSTONEPRESS.COM
SUNSTONE PRESS / POST OFFICE BOX 2321 / SANTA FE, NM 87504-2321 /USA
(505) 988-4418 / ORDERS ONLY (800) 243-5644 / FAX (505) 988-1025

For Patricia, Genesee, and Riley

Contents

1

Early Signs

First...

...we gain weight...

...find gray hairs...

...we receive new kinds of mail...

... we dribble...

... attract stains and crumbs...

...the young call you "sir" and offer you a seat.

2

What Do We Lose?

Old friends names...

...glasses, cell phone...   ...keys...

24

...wallet...

...forget to zip our zipper...

...and go to the other room but can't remember why.

We lose our hearing...

... so we miss the punch line.

You may consider a hearing aid...

...or go with "selective hearing."

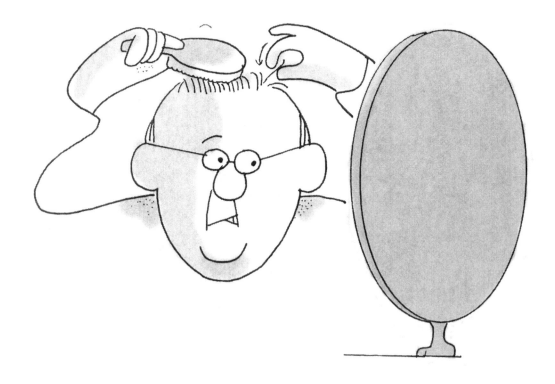

There's hair...

...height...

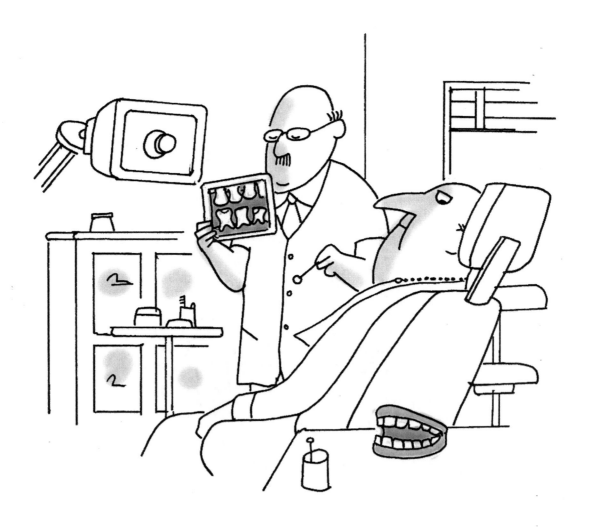

...teeth...

...sight...

...muscle...

...balance...

...dexterity.

We drop things...

...and the plumbing goes south.

3

Challenges

Frequent trips to the john...

... so we improvise...

...and take risks.

Other challenges include…

...the undergarments...

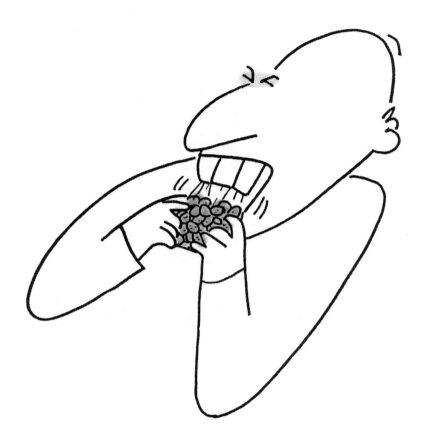

...a pack of nuts...

...a jar...

...blood pressure...

...arthritis...

...dressing...

...and getting out of your chair...

... crossing the street...

... what button to push...

...bending over...

...a young wife...

...gas control...

...removing guests at bedtime...

... communication with the family...

...new phones...

... and diets.

4

Spare Time

When the party's over...

...what does one do with all the spare time?

Join a gym...

...try golf...

...travel...

... go back to school...

... have a political discussion...

...have lunch with the guys...

...take up cooking...

... watch the weather...

...or go to movies in the afternoon.

Wait for mail...

...organize pills...

...garden...

...help the wife shop...

... share humorous emails...

...post reminder notes...

...wait for sleep...

I can't sleep!

did I lock the door?

what should I wear to the party?

Who cares? stupid party!

is the dog in?

I won't go to the stupid party

The plumber.. I'm sure the S.O.B overcharged me!

I hate parties! Maybe I better go

is the gas off?

Now I'm worried!

Now I'm really stressed

I can't sleep!

99

...read the obits...

...fix things...

... have a mid-life crisis...

103

...and sleep a lot.

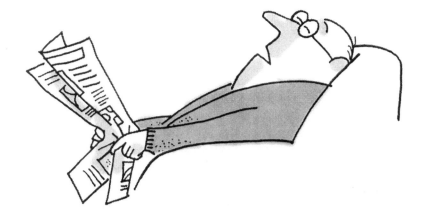

5

Things to Avoid

A major spat...

...repeating your favorite stories...

111

...school reunions...

... becoming a living treasure...

...remembering when...

...new technology...

... stairs...

...large SUVs...

... small cars with high curbs...

...an untied shoe lace...

...large recliners...

...ladders...

...bathtubs...

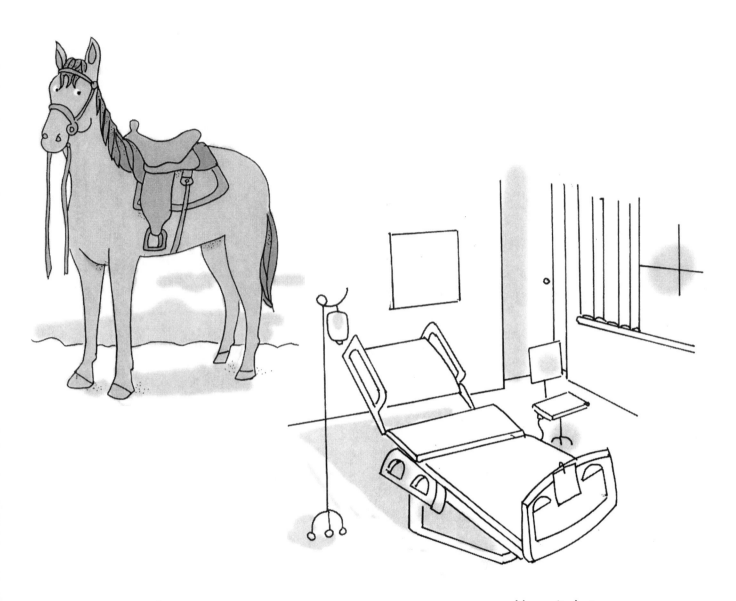

...horses...

...and hospital stays.

6

What We Become

Dirty old men...

... stubborn...

...dependent...

... on others...

... until finally we become a... curmudgeon.

CPSIA information can be obtained
at www.ICGtesting.com
Printed in the USA
LVOW09s0112271016
510468LV00030B/494/P